T0086156

REVOLUTIONARY
DIARY

REVOLUTIONARY DIARY

DIARY

Thoughts of a C.A.G.E.D. Mind

Saadi Williams/Kareka Thomas-Hargrove

REVOLUTIONARY DIARY
THOUGHTS OF A C.A.G.E.D. MIND

Copyright © 2022 Saadi Williams/Kareka Thomas-Hargrove.

All rights reserved. No part of this book may be used or reproduced by any means, graphic, electronic, or mechanical, including photocopying, recording, taping or by any information storage retrieval system without the written permission of the author except in the case of brief quotations embodied in critical articles and reviews.

iUniverse books may be ordered through booksellers or by contacting:

iUniverse
1663 Liberty Drive
Bloomington, IN 47403
www.iuniverse.com
844-349-9409

Because of the dynamic nature of the Internet, any web addresses or links contained in this book may have changed since publication and may no longer be valid. The views expressed in this work are solely those of the author and do not necessarily reflect the views of the publisher, and the publisher hereby disclaims any responsibility for them.

Any people depicted in stock imagery provided by Getty Images are models, and such images are being used for illustrative purposes only.
Certain stock imagery © Getty Images.

Foreword & Editing, Kareka Thomas-Hargrove

ISBN: 978-1-6632-3910-5 (sc)
ISBN: 978-1-6632-3911-2 (e)

Library of Congress Control Number: 2022908311

Print information available on the last page.

iUniverse rev. date: 07/22/2022

DEDICATION

I dedicate this book to my amazing daughter Majesty. Always remember princess, it doesn't matter where you're at in life you can accomplish great things. Work hard, determined to beat the odds you're up against and be sure of yourself the whole way.

Revolutionary Diary:
Thoughts of C.A.G.E.D Mind

Saadi Williams

INTRODUCTION

This diary of poems will show you the world through the eyes of a caged man. The author of this dairy embarked on a journey to share his gift with others back in 2009. His poems filled his readers with inspiration, motivation, and love. One of his goals in life is to share his gift with the rest of the world. As you read the first part of his diary, allow him to take you on a journey through his mind. He hopes while you're on this journey you will feel inspired, motivated, and loved.

CHAPTER 1

MIND OVER MATTER

Against all odds I prevail…

Freedom Song

For some people prison can be a tomb, For others it can be a school of thought. I've seen this place break men spiritually, mentally, and physically. At an early age I refused to be counted among the broken men. I rebel against the concept of becoming a lesser man when I can become a better man.

This poem represents what people see when they see me. They wonder how I do it or how I can remain so strong. For me, life without parole doesn't mean the end. Life without parole means I have to engage into a fight that'll give my life reason, purpose, and cause.

I often tell people I didn't understand life until they took my life. So far I've done what I suppose to under the circumstances I've elevated myself, I've established hope where they said it was none. I plan to continue fighting and resisting the constant pressure I'm under. I'm determined to beat the odds by showing them what they considered to be my ending was really my beginning.

"Freedom Song"

I listen to the song the caged bird sing

I wonder why the song so sweet

How can he smile through his melody

with chains on his Feet

A capitalist society downing him

Barbed Wire Fences surrounding him

The baptist want to drown him

But…...

His Family crown him

They took him From his land

They clipped his wings so he cant Fly away

They labeled him a Blackbird

They erased his old time grace

They tried to cover up his legacy

But….

What's lost is never forgotten

In a rebellions mind

Bowing down is never a option

They can't break his spirit

He is determined to get free

Now.….

I understand why He song the caged bird sung is so sweet

<u>Where am I</u>

For the people who have experienced prison you understand this poem clearly. For the people who have not experienced prison I want you to use your imagination for a moment.

Imagine what it's like living in a place built on a foundation of guilt, misery, and sorrow. The abnormal becomes normal, everyday you witness oppression. Negativity is like a black cloud consuming the sky of your world. It's dangerous, it's overwhelming, it's easy to give in, it's easy to give up.

It takes a certain type of person to raise above it all and make something of themselves. There's no way to avoid it, it's right in your face everywhere you turn. The only thing you can do is dig deep inside your soul and find strength, find light, and find something to hold on too.

Without a doubt, it's easier said than done. When your life's on the line and your success depends on your survival the decision shouldn't be hard to make.

"Where am I"

Gray skies

Wet grass

Brick buildings

Barb Wire fences

Where am I?

Dark clouds

Dim Lights

Dark thoughts

Shattered souls

Where am I?

Broken hearts

Misery

Sorrow

No love

No conscience

No hope for tomorrow

Where am I?

Secluded

Confined

Held back

Counted out

Where am I?

Fights

Wars

Violence

murder

Where am I?

Corruption

Betrayal

Conquest

Lies

Where am I?

Against all odds

Locked down

Chained up

Cold

Where am I?

I'm in No man's land

Where authority is abused

Where majority is confused

Where the weak suffer

Where the strong struggle

Where reality is rougher

So

Staying out of trouble is tougher

Yet and still

I survive

I overcome

I will make it out

When will it end

When I was 22 and 23 I questioned every significant part of me.
I wanted to make sure I was ready to commit myself to a lifelong
journey. A journey that would consist of trials, tribulation, mistakes,
and mental anguish; as well as a host of other growing pains.

I wasn't afraid I just wanted to be sure I was dedicating myself to the right thing. At one point I was numb. At one point I could not differentiate between my pain and happiness because they felt the same. I was vicious and despite my numbness I knew I didn't want to be remembered that way.

When I questioned myself I answered honestly, I didn't allow my ego to answer for me. The answer showed me who I am, what I'm capable of, and who I could become. This was a pivotal point in my life. From that moment until now I haven't turned back. I understood in order to appreciate the rise I had to experience the fall.

"When Will it End"

When will it end?

When will I start

Why can't the sun shine in a world so dark?

Am I great as I say I am?

Am I all that I know I can be?

How can I not be vainglorious If My Ego is the definition of ME?

It's not hard as we make it

It's not easy as it seem

I have problems distinguishing my nightmares From my Dream

Nevertheless

I know when it will end

Because

I know when i'll start

Living underground is why the sun can't shine in a world so dark

I am who I am

What more can I be

I'm not vainglorious so My Expression is the definition of Me

We make it when its hard

So they think it's easy

Keep your eyes open

Nightmares and Dreams are products of sleeping

<u>Misery</u>

Misery has many faces and I've seen a few of them. Being hit with so much at one time can be devastating. Misery accompanied me the most in the beginning of my incarceration. I couldn't find a better way so I let my discomfort and emotional distress get the best of me.

When I say "misery manipulates the weak and takes advantage of my vulnerability." Misery made my weakness look violent and my vulnerability seem dominant. Trutfully, I was in a dark mental block and misery loved my company at that time.

I didn't realize how miserable I was until someone close to me told me I was becoming a "MONSTER". Me a "MONSTER". IMPOSSIBLE! When I think of a monster I think of something hideous and harmful. That was not me and I couldn't believe that was how I seem to the world. It focused me to face the man in the mirror.

During that moment of realization the stage was set for my transformation. I would no longer terrorize, hurt others, or myself. I learned how to deal with my emotions. I became the man who taught the boy.

"Misery"

Walk with me

Let me tell you about a girl named Misery

She hates being lonely

SHe hates being ignored

Her passion is pain

Despair is Her burning desire

She's a bad girl

Addicted to grief

Influenced by misfortune

Driven by sorrow

I met her in the school of Hard knocks

The struggle turned me on to her

She's the type of girl that'll bring the worst out you

Make you want to scream Fuck the world

I told you

She's a Bad Girl

She takes advantage of the vulnerable

She manipulates the weak

She despises you strong

She'll destroy you if you let her

She Dangerous

Im telling you this because she loves company

She Loves Attention

Be careful

She'll get in your head

Hate

A lot of my poetry started out as a reminder to myself to stay focused. At times it's so easy to get distracted and lose our way. The last 13 years of my life have been full of drama, wars, envy, jealousy, hate, lies, oppression, etc. Of course, there were moments when I deviated.

As people we all have a certain way we learn. For me that way is through experience and observation. This was actually written while

I was doing 2 years in solitary confinement. I told myself I was too smart, too capable, and too determined to be consumed by madness.

When we wake up in the morning we have to know that there's a possibility we'll be tested by some type of addiction. We have to prepare ourselves mentally. There is no set rule saying 'this says you're free from trials." My advice to you is if it occurs don't let it stop you. Hopefully you woke up with an agenda, and stay the course.

"Hate"

Hate can't stop the sun From shining

Lies can't stop the earth from spinning

Wars can't stop the seasons From changing

Oppression can't stop the Force of Gravity

Constraint can't stop the Flow of the Ocean

Jealousy can't stop the Law of Attraction

Fear can't stop the Law of Destiny

Envy can't stop karma

Prison can't stop thought

None of these things can stop universal Law

So…..

Why let any of it stop you

<u>Can you see it</u>

About 11 years ago I started doing something that changed my life. Once a week I make time to reflect on my strong and weak points. I call it a character building session. It gives me the opportunity to see myself, my light, my highs, my lows, my good, and my bad.

This type of reflection is good for every aspect of you. It's good for your spirit, it's good for your mind, and it's good for your body. It really shows you where you are and where you need to be. It's a for sure way to consistently get better until you reach the pinnacle of yourself.

In my opinion, if I'm willing to spend thousands of dollars to go to the finest colleges, why can't I spend time studying by myself? Prison has given me the ability to look deep inside myself to search myself.

I've seen my blind side and ignorance. I've seen when I've enslaved myself (mentally) by refusing to break through the illusionary walls I placed around myself. I've seen the wickedness I adopted now I'm holding on to the peace I've found.

Take advantage of every moment you have to look inward. Don't be egotistical, prideful, or biased about it. Be honest about what you see. Use this technique to build character and become a better version of yourself. Over time you'll begin to see two people, the person you were and the person you have become.

"Can you see it"

Can you see it

Can you see the love

Can you see the pain

Can you see the Truth

Can you see the Lies

Can you see the Peace

Can you see the War

Can you see the Freedom

Can you see the Slavery

Can you see the Justice

Can you see the Wickedness

Can you see the Struggle

Can you see the Mountain

Can you see the Valley

Can you see the Knowledge

Can you see the Ignorance

Can you see the Wisdom

Can you see the Foolishness

Can you see the Understanding

Can you see the Blindness

Can you see the Walls

Can you see the doors

If you can't

You should study yourself more often

<u>**Understand**</u>

Hopelessness is the fire that burns down the city of faith. When you live in a place full of resentment it's so easy to become a product of the environment. I have first hand experience with this. When I say "it is anger in every corner.., vengeance in every heart" I lived. When I say "corruption is easy.., betrayal is natural" I was a victim of it all .

At one point in my incarceration I was the kid with no hope. That led to rage that polluted the air and the mayhem that was peaking through the window. I often tell people one of the most dangerous things in the world is a black man that don't give a fuck. I know that because I've been him, and what fueled my everyday life was hopelessness.

When I write about the effect and life of prison I often use the term dark world. That's not by mistake, sometimes negativity can be so overbearing your world can seem gloomy. It's like being in a black hole. The gravitational pull is so strong light can't escape, it's not the blackhole and light escapes; I'm proof of that.

"Understand"

What can I do

In a world so dark

It's anger in every corner

Vengeance in every heart

All you see is envy green eyes glaring at you

Jealousy knocking at your door

Mayhem peaking in your window

Rage pollutes the air

The foul smell affects everyday

corruption is easy

Betrayal is natural

It's cold

There's no safe place

There's no boundaries

All lines get crossed

We're fenced in

We're locked away

What can I do

In this world dark as shadows

I can shine

I can bring light

I can show everyone what they've been missing

CHAPTER 2

L.I.F.E.

Learning is For Everybody

*"As Long we continue to learn
we'll continue to grow."*

Life lessons pt. 1

When I made the decision to change my life for the better I believe that when I truly started to live my life. They say a 1,000 mile journey starts with the first step. Change was surely the first step for me.

My next step was learning myself and unfolding into who I have the potential to be. In a short amount of years I experienced so much it was staggering. While writing this diary taught me to prepare myself. It taught me how to preserve and stay focused on my goals.

As I say in the poem winners don't quit, Quitters don't win. Things don't always go according to plan, but that doesn't mean we are supposed to give up; especially when it's something we're striving to accomplish. This far life has instilled in me grit, grind, and ambition. I believe what's worth having is worth sacrificing for.

Remember in every mistake there's a lesson, learn from it and implement it in your life immediately. I put emphasis on immediately because a mistake only occurs once (that's your learning moment). After that if you do that same thing again it's not a mistake it's your fault. Keep that in mind as you do your thing.

"Life Lessons Pt. 1"

In this world

We will experience the Good, the Bad, and the Ugly

Knowing this

Prepare yourself For All

Expect Test

Expect Trials and Tribulations

No Matter what

Be Effective

Be Strong

Remember!

Winners don't Quit, Quitters don't win

Remember!

You get what you earn

Expect nothing more

Skills make the good Good

Hard Work, Determination, and Commitment makes the great Great

What do you want to be?

How Far are you willing to go?

What are you willing to sacrifice?

Answer Honestly......

Make Moves

Don't Make excuses

Don't Deviate

Stay the course

If you want it

<u>Win Win</u>

Of course like most people I've had my share of setbacks. During those moments my favorite mantra is "Don't focus on the set back, Focus on the come back".

One of the many things I've learned in prison is how to be efficient under pressure. At times people come after you, they watch you, and they antagonize you. They want you to fail and they'll do whatever they can to accomplish that goal. It's sad but it's true. Over the years I've had people work with administration against me, plant things in my locker, spread gossip, and try to turn people against me. Nevertheless I'm making the most of the 24 hours Allah blessed me with. Despite all of that I stand tall and continue to strive for greatness. The path I'm on has its own challenges, and those are challenges I'm waiting to face. Iwant allow adversity to keep me from being victorious. I see it, I feel it, and I'm not going against it.

In this poem what I'm saying to you is: Figure out what you want to do with your life.

See it clearly with your mind's eye and don't let anything stop you. Even if you don't accomplish it the first time you'll gain experience for the next time. Give your life purpose because a life without purpose isn't a life at all, it's just more existence.

"Win Win"

Strive!!!!!

Know what you want

See it clear

Don't be afraid to take chances

Don't be afraid to learn

Embrace the process

When goals are taking serious they evolve into accomplishments

Remember…

Mistakes are inevitable

Just make sure they're not careless

Do what needs to be done

Question what needs to be questioned

Adhere to what's Favorable

Disregard what's Detrimental

Believe…

See the Victory

See the Adversity

Feel it in your soul

Beat everything you're up against

At least attempt too

Focus…

It's only 2 options

Win

Or

Learn

Live

Life is like a roller coaster; it has its highs and lows as well as its twists and turns. It can go from exciting to scary in a matter of seconds. Some people enjoy the experience while others dread it. All in all it's a ride we'll never forget.

Unlike your typical roller coaster when this ride is over it's over. It's no such thing as getting back in line and doing it all over again; the end is final. You'll be held accountable for what you do on this ride. People win, remember the way you express yourself and the way you act, the high and low points. Be mindful of that.

If this poem was a person it would be the kind of person it would be the kind of person that has an achievers attitude and an outgoing personality. In my early 20's I was among a very solid group of guys.

We learned from each other everyday. I remember telling them "Life is what ya make it, it's not what you want it to be." I still live by that.

Life was given to us as a gift. Like all other gifts we're supposed to appreciate it and make the most of it. We're not supposed to take it for granted. If a guy in prison fighting to overturn a life sentence can use strengths and capabilities to turn his ideas into reality, so can you.

As I said "Life is the ultimate test"..."its hands on…" Turn it into something special; something worth remembering. Whether you're high or low, be the best version of yourself. Be intentional about your success. Do it by purpose not by accident.

"Live"

Your life is the Ultimate test

Its hands on

It's about the choice you make

It's about the chance you take

It's about how quick you learn

It's about what you do with what you learn

Why be average when you can be above it

Why lack when you can excel

Be cautious about what you accept

Be mindful of what you do

Your actions determine your worth

However

You determine your actions

Your life is the Ultimate test

For some it's easy For some it's hard

Regardless of the situation

Do your best

Don't let other people's limitation becomes your

Don't let success destroy you

Don't let error define you

Be Quick to recover

Be humble

Take the Right risk

Stay focus

I Promise

It's easier said than done

<u>Weighs of Approach</u>

Coming of age in prison was like rising through the ranks of a scholastic system. You will be taught and you will be tested. In many situations the margin for error is very small. Alhamdulillah I had some great teachers and one of the most important lessons they taught me was how to approach.

The art of approach is fundamental in every person's life. Most of my success started with approach. Whether it was a goal, establishing peace, speaking to a crowd, or establishing bonds and relationships the way I initiated it spoke volumes.

In this poem I mention phases like "Intentions are everything", "proceed with purpose", "Don't get in your own way" and "Don't procrastinate". Take all of it into consideration because it all counts. We can be our biggest asset or we can be our biggest inability, the choice is yours.

If you're a play maker then you know what I'm saying is true. If you want to become a playmaker, study the weights of approach.

"Weighs of Approach"

In critical situations

Weight your options of approach

Confidence is essential

Awareness is fundamental

Intentions are everything

Proceed with purpose

Don't stumble over your own feet

Don't get in your own way

Maintain a productive pace

Pay attention!!!

Details are game changers

Consider your strengths

Make the necessary moves

Don't over think

Don't underestimate

Don't procrastinate

Be committed

Why approach timid

Don't be apprehensive

Be certain

Be Precise

Be Mindful

Be Ready!

Be willing!!

Knowledge is Power

My quest for knowledge began in December of 2010, I was 22 years old. This is when I saw I had the ability to retain, convey, and apply information effectively. This is also when I saw possessing knowledge is possessing power and with that power came leadership, responsibility, and accountability.

In my opinion, one of the greatest gifts Allah gave to man is the ability to learn. In taking the time to learn I have become a better person. Learning motivates me to motivate others. I refuse to go back to my days of ignorance.

When you break down the word ignorance the root word is ignored. To ignore is not to know, to ignore is to disregard. In that context to be ignorant would be to go against what you know.

It does not matter what stage of your life you're in, there's always room for improvement. The more knowledge you have the more versatile and flexible you can be. Knowledge is like wealth. Share it with the needy, they'll appreciate it.

"Knowledge is Power"

Time is Precious

Make every moment count For something

Your next move is just as important as your next breath

Breath easy….

Take nothing For Granted

A minor advantage can cause a major victory

Versatility is Golden

Flexibility is Favorable

You know about the one eyed man

He's a King in the land of the Blind

His superiority come From being able to see what others can't

Therefore

His level of awareness is beyond their comprehension

His moves are more precise

His plans are more efficient

Simply because

He know what others don't

Knowledge is Power

Obtain it

Do the Right thing with it

Use it to put yourself in a beneficial position

Be a Giant in a world full of Midgets

Stand taller

See Further

Have a bigger Impact

Don't waste your time

In this poem I wanted to put emphasis on how valuable time really is. There were moments in my life when I tok time for granted. I didn't see how precious it was. I didn't think about death so I didn't think about my time being limited.

Now I live with a sense of urgency. My life has more purpose, I'm focused on leaving a legacy. Time waits for no one when it's gone, it's gone. Individuals should be conscious of the fact that our time is limited. We should be more careful about how time is spent, how time is shared, how time is invented, and how time is enjoyed.

Your life is yours to do whatever you please with it. Just keep in mind your time is limited. It's 24 hours in a day which equals 3600 minutes so make your time count for something.

"Don't waste your time"

They say time is Money

Therefore

Invest in tit

Buy into it

Share it

Enjoy it

Just Dont waste it

Be Careful

Be Responsible

Don't spend it all in one place

Spread your wealth

Put some here

Place some there

Make sure it's Beneficial

Make sure it's worthwhile

In this world

Today becomes tomorrow and Tomorrow becomes yesterday

Your time is valuable

Like Money

Everyone want more than they already have

But it's not that simple

When your time runs out its gone

You can't get it back

Be smart

The Goal is to do your very best with the time you have

Life lessons pt. 2

Since I was an adolescent my life has been anything but normal. The things I've seen I can't un-seen, the things I've done and can't undo. It's truly amazing to me to see how far I've come. My mentality is much different. It's like the man I am and the boy I was are 2 different people from 2 different times.

The thoughts I express in this poem is sincere advice to the reader. I didn't learn this from a book, a speech, or a class. I learned this from life experiences that I like to call "life lessons".

It hasn't been sweet but it has been worth it. I had to learn some lessons the hard way but it made me a better person. All my life I hated people giving me direction or guidance. I didn't want to listen. Everything I've been through at this point in my life has put me in the position to share my journey with you. I made the mistakes so you wouldn't have too.

"Life Lesson Pt. 2"

In life

You get what you earn

Expect nothing more

Time reveal All

Patience and preservation is key

To be Patient doesn't mean to Procrastinate

To Preserve doesn't mean to merely withstand

Being Patient is staying Poised

Perseverance is having the ability to endure and maintain

Be focused

Don't let disappointment discourage you

Instead

Let it push you beyond your limit

Your life is your Responsibility

No one else can live it For you

It's what you make it

Make it Magnificent, make it legendary, make it memorable

Or

Make it Worthless

It's your choice

Defy the odds against you

The strong stand tall

The Weak Fall Short

Hunting Season

When it comes to accomplishing my goals and executing my plans this is my attitude. Too many times great ideas are pushed aside because someone gave up. My circumstances have taught me to go after what I want while I'm able. I got tired of saying I could've done that or I had the chance to do that. Truth is the opportunity means nothing if you do nothing with it.

In so many ways tracking accomplishments is like hunting. Timing is a factor, positioning yourself in the right place is a factor, and most of all having patience is a factor. The opportunity will present itself then you have to take advantage. How many times in our life have we said we wanted to do something and the opportunity came and we weren't ready. We simply let that opportunity pass us by.

...t is so much for us to accomplish in this world. We all have our own skill sets and capabilities to contribute to humanity. Lets first develop ourselves then lets hunt for opportunities to be great.

"Hunting Season"

Take Aim!

Shoot!

You Miss

Shoot Again

Keep shooting!

Be More Accurate

Its Hunting Season

Be Alert

Be watchful

Be ready

We looking For Opportunity

She can be anywhere

She the Queen of the Jungle

Everybody searching For her

Some will find her

But…..

Only a few will know what to do with her

The fool is intimidated by her beauty

The weak is mesmerized by her Grace

She's one of a kind

When it come to survival

She make a difference

Don't- Blink

Shhh......

Listen

There She Go

"See it For what it is"

Cash rules everything around me

But……..

IF Money is an illusion what is everything around me

What seems to be is what seems to be

Therefore

It'll never last

Because it SEEMS to be

Money make the Poor happy and make the Rich cry

It makes a man steal and makes a women lie

What's the outcome of good in a evil heart

What's the outcome of evil in Good hands

Many will die For a dollar before they die For their momma

Priorities are misplaced

Desire is chosen over Honor

Is the price of Fame more valuable than your life

Does justice make your heart cold because it's Just- ice

Or is it just us?

Too much salt raise your Blood Pressure

Too much oppression make your blood Rush

Money is everything to those seeking material gain

Money is a tool to those seeking to make a change

Money is like a pawn on the chess board

Make your next move your best move

Always remember

Only in a race For the worst will the best lose

"When you're right"

When you know you're right let no one tell you're wrong

When you know you're wrong let no one tell you're right

Live according to what you know

If you know better do better

In every mistake there's a lesson

Search For it

The World is a classroom

Experience is a Teacher

Pay Attention

Look Listen and Observe

Don't get caught up in words

You can be whatever you choose to be

Be Yourself

Be Careful

Be Exceptional

Be the one that make a difference

Why be anything else

Why spill a cup Full of seconds

Why waste time

Bobby said seize it

Tell yourself you can do it and believe it

Be Humbled when you achieve it

Men measure men by action

Words are For the Blind to comprehend 'Establish a Firm Foundation

Stand on it til the End

"Brave heart"

A man with no intergrity is a man with no Morale

A Man with no principles is a man with no Morals

Respect is vital

The Man loved For what he has dies powerless

The Man loved For who he is die Honored

Your character is Fundamental

Your conduct speak for itself

Protect your dignity

Sometimes being in the worst situations can bring the best at you

Sometimes being in the best situations can bring the worst out you

Make sure your cornerstone is Firm

Establish a code to live by

Go against it For no one

Never compromise your creed or code of ethics

Be as righteous as you can be in every situation

Stand for something

Establish Goals

Engage in Pursuit

Blaze a Trail

Be the BEst you

No one lives Forever

Death is a Promise

CHAPTER 3

R.I.S.E

Revolution Inspire Strength Education

'You weren't given a voice to be afraid of it'

<u>Erica</u>

Before a house can be built the foundation must be laid. All parts of the foundation are essential to the structure. The foundation must be solid enough to withstand any threat, sabotage, or vandalism. Without the foundation the house can't stand.

As a black man I see American history from a different point of view. When most people think of America they think of being free and the opportunity to chase the American Dream. For me, that is not so, I think of what my people went through especially women.

I believe neither skin color or cultural background determine if one person is more dominant or superior than another. I'm not a black supremacist, my agenda is not to make. Black Americans are the ruling class over all other Americans. I'm not a Domestic Terrorist have no desire to attack the American people.

I'm a man who found it's hard to ignore his passion to speak his mind. The system established to govern this country needs to be rebuilt from the ground up before there can be freedom, justice, and equality.

Racism, slavery, and prejudice are some of the evil essentails mixed into the foundation of this nation. Like a building that needs to be re-done. If people tear down the structure and rebuild on the e foundation it doesn't matter how different the structure looks,

s standing on the same thing it stood on before.

Erica

Erica was raped at an early age

In the Aftermath

She lost her sanity

Her natural aura became an object of desire

In this new beginning

Only the selected could eat at her table

Everyone else was said to be Filthy and unworthy

Some were ran off

Others were broken

All in the name of Erica

The pain she Felt began to show on the surface

The doctors wouldn't heal her

To them she was worth more in a sick state

Common people tried to help her despite the Doctors negligence

But…..

They were deemed Black devils

They were either Jailed or casted out

If not killed

She screamed in pain as they branded her with 50 scars

They wrote songs about her

other women around the world envied her wealth

They were too busy looking at her appearance

They couldn't see what she was going through on the inside

The murders

The Rapes

The oppression

The Poor state of mind

The history

One night she had a dream

She was being judged for who she became

They asked her over and over again

Who are you?

Who are you?

She began to shed tears

She began to shake uncontrollably

She looked the judge in the face

She said

I AM Erica

Choose a side

When I wrote this poem I knew what the rest of my life would consist of. I knew I wanted to make a change. I knew I wanted to make a difference in my environment as well as society at large. I knew I wanted to have a positive impact on someone if not everyone.

Even in this microcosmic world we call prison I saw how influential I can be. Alot of officers and administrators said I taught hate. They considered me to be an instigator or an antagonizer. To them I was a trouble maker because at that time not only was I a charismatic gang member who used his influence to open people's eyes to what was done to them and to what was being to them.

Over time I took it upon myself to change my focus and show my fellow brothers the way. I have been teaching my new way of living. I've shown them how to rebel against the status quo by revolutionizing and reforming themselves through education, unification, and demonstration.

"Choose a side"

What happened to Liberation?

What happened to Power to the People?

Was our Revolutionary spirit assassinated in Prison with George?

Was it Murdered in the street with Huey P?

My Father is Disgraced

My Mother is Suffering

My Brothers and sisters show no Respect

Me and my brothers and sisters have to do something

They Tail to Display Honor in Race Ride

How can we be wrong for fighting for what's right?

Blood has to be shed

Pain has to be Felt

The Victory has to be Pure

Survival is a most

You eat or you get ate

You rebel or you Bow down

The strong survive the weak Die

Choose a side

Pillars of a Liberator

I didn't appreciate freedom or desire to be a liberator until I experienced being chained up and locked down. Oppression and injustice were just words until circumstances taught me their meaning. WHat we go throught has a very meticulous way of molding us into who we are, and for that reason I'm thankful.

Liberation gives us hope, it gives us a reason to believe and look forward to tomorrow. It gives our lives purpose and strengthens the people. I know now I don't do what I do for myself. I do it for those who can't do it themselves. I also do it for those who will be after me. If I don't do my part in establishing the pillars of the liberator who will.

My struggle began the day I was born. Paths were set for me to choose from and standards were set for me to aspire too. At 7 if you asked me about my future or what I believe in I wouldn't have too much to say. At 33 I can answer that with passion, detail, and commitment. The real question is will I live to see that future before I die for what I believe in.

"Pillars of a Liberator"

Liberation is Action

Liberation is Resistance

Liberation is Sacrifice

Liberation is Freedom

Liberation is Justice

Liberation is Inspiration

Liberation is Motivation

Liberation is why we struggle

Liberation is why we Breath

Liberation is the Force

Liberation is the solution

Liberation is not the Dream after the Nightmare

Liberation is the cause of the effect

Liberation is not what the thoughtless think

Liberation is more than existence

Liberation is to be Alive

Liberation is Independence

Liberation is Self-Defense

<u>Let's</u>

I'm speaking to the revolutionizers and the reformers. Those who believe a better way is possible and are willing to do their part in achieving it. The change begins with us. Let's start with ourselves, the people around us, and the environment we're in.

When we as people feel our government is not doing right by us it's up to us to make changes. The first change should occur with our mentality. For so long people have been taught what to think instead of how to think. A Lot of people's opinions are not their own. They let the media and the people in power think for them. Even when they feel it's not right they go along with it because that is the overall view of the majority.

America is a melting pot full of different ethnicities, creeds, races, ideas, and etc. Despite our differences we all have to co- exist with each other. We have to find a common ground, things we can agree on and unite around. I believe one of those things is a New America. An America we can all benefit from and truly participate in.

"Let's"

Let's influence a culture

Let's change our environment

Let's change our society

Let's...

Lets base our mentality off reality

Let's see with clarity

Let's stop falling victim

Let's rise to the occasion

Why make excuses?

Why blame somebody else?

Why discredit yourself?

Lets merge unity with purpose

Lets separate ourselves from ignorance

Let's be a light for the next generation

Let's make history

Let's do it!!!

Let's do what they think we can't do

Let's succeed

Let's overcome

Let's be the answer to the people's prayer

Change is inevitable

What we do today will be talked about tomorrow

Lets live like it

Let's start now

Lets...

Character of a Nation

The history of the Blackwall street in Tulsa, Oklahoma will always be a source of inspiration for me. What those brothers and sisters did in that era of America was amazing. Against the odds and against the times, they found a way to band together and thrive. They created a culture of success, self-reliance, and unity.

The adversity didn't cripple them, it didn't petrify them. They didn't make excuses or place blame. They saw things for what they were and they did what they had to do in order to make things better for themselves. Of course, that fueled more hate than love. What they did then is a blueprint for us now. This is the opportunity for us to create an identity for ourselves. An identity that consists of strength, perseverance, resilience, revolution, unity, success, and true

ood. Yes, it will take work, it will take time, and it will take
..ifices. It could possibly take some of our lives, but I believe in
ne end it will be worth it.

"Character of a Nation"

Unity in the Face of Adversity define the character of a Nation

We Fight

We Grind

We Survive

We refuse to be counted among the broken men

We refuse to be stepped on

We refuse to be slept on

We refuse to let another man choose our destiny

We refuse to be a victim

To the struggle

To the pain

To the odds

Let your mind mold society

Don't let society mold your mind

Be about P.E.A.C.E

Propagating Education And Changing Environments

Protecting Each Other Against this Corrupt Establishment

One hand wash the other

I Help you

You Help me

We Help each other

U-N-I verse All

The climax of resistance is revolution

Sometime that's the only resolution

Kill For a Purpose

Die For a Cause

Real Talk

Until the political representatives listen to the grassroots representatives the American problem will never be solved. To see the root of problems you have to be where the problems are. The people in power see it on t.v. they don't see it in their front yard, at the corner store, or in the neighborhood it happens in. They don't understand the traumatizing effect it can have on a child. They don't feel the hopelessness of the elders or the rage of the youth. They never will until they listen to us.

Political representatives are not talking about the problems, they are talking around the problems. After a problem is discussed the agreed upon solution comes next. Because of oaths they took, their hands are tied. They can only do so much because they can't go against the oath they swore to uphold.

This conversation is way overdue. We need to speak about the unadulterated truth. Not being politically correct or edited for t.v. We tried going to talk to them now they need to come talk to us.

"Real Talk"

We want Real Talk

Let's talk about Racism Let's talk about the culture

Let's talk about the History Let's talk about the vultures

Let's talk about the Pain Let's talk about the struggle

Let's talk about the Hate Let's talk about the Muzzle

Let's talk Politics Let's talk violence

Let's have a raw conversation about sensitive Topics

We want Real Talk!

Let's talk about society, Let's talk about why the police eyeing me

When I say "Me" I mean the Minorities in American

Subject to be stopped and searched because the Majority scared of US

Let's talk about the crime rate Let's talk about the mind state

Let's talk about a system that can't define race but try to save Face

Let's talk about the Love and Respect they tried to erase

We want Real Talk!

Let's talk about the Pretending and all the Fake well wishing

Let's talk about poverty let's talk about addiction

Let's talk about the Women let's talk about Children

Let's talk about the parents being trapped inside of Prison

Let's have a raw conversation to clarify people vision

We want Real Talk!

Let's talk about the unadulterated Truth no matter how much it hurt

Sensitizing people feelings make the situation worst

Are you scared?

Because the Resolution will be a Revolution Full of purpose and passion

Are you scared?

Because people will start taking and enforcing

instead of demanding and asking

Are you scared?

Because it'll make people Aware of your diversionary tactics

or, are you scared?

Because Real Talk provoke real Action

<u>Why America</u>

When I see pictures of men and women hanging from trees or children being held in chains like animals, my blood boils. When I think of the men, women, and children who were beaten because they didn't want to be slaves my soul cries out for justice. When I see men, women, and children being killed in the streets by the police I say to myself "why America".

The process of my anscestors becoming slaves was brutal. They were stolen and transported like cargo. They were beaten and broken down to their lowest state. Think about that… women and children were forced to watch as the strongest men were killed. All of this for what?

Some say let history be history, but how can I when America hasn't been held accountable for what they did. History tells us about the murders, rapes, and other hienous crimes that no one had to answer for. An open apology or attempt to fix something is not the same thing as being held accountable. We were not brought here to be citizens with rights. Throughout American history so many great men and women were killed for standing up for themselves.

With this poem I'm asking the universal question "Why"? Why did they do what they did? WHy haven't they been held accountable? Why are minorities still being treated like second class citizens? Why do we have to fight so hard to be recognized as people with rights that need to be respected? Why?

'Why America"

Why do you hate me?
Why did you rape my mother?
Why did you murder my father?
Why did you take my brother?

Why did you trap my sister?

Why?

Why do you push me to the ground?

Why do you put your knee in my neck?

Why do you press harder when I say "I can't breathe"?

Why do you want to kill me?

Why can't I live my life?

Why can't I wear a hoodie at night?

Why?

Why are you so quick to arrest me?

Why are you so quick to reject me?

Why am I the embodiment of evil?

Why do I have to fight to show you I'm equal?

Why do I have to scream for my life to matter?

Why do I have to protect?

Why did I have to boycott to sit where you sit?

Why did I have to risk my freedom to eat where you eat?

Why did you manipulate me with what you preach?

Why?

Why did you hate Malcolm?

What was wrong with Noble Drew Ali?

Why was Marcus a problem?

Why did you kill Martin?

Why was Nat Turner a murder?

What was the problem with the panther's?

Why is it so hard to give answers?

Why did you create CointelPro?

Why were you afraid of a "Black Messiah"?

Why did you say the U.S. was created for the people by the people?

When?

In Reality

Your people didn't see my people as people

Why?

<u>Galvanized</u>

The truth hurts who it offends. When it comes to making a change or establishing a new way, the only people who will be against it are the ones who want to keep things the same. Most people want to maintain a position of power. The rest either lack the will to make sacrifices or they're simply afraid of change. If you are among that group this is not for you.

When I see the news I see the discussion and disappointment of the people. When I listen to politicians I hear the false promises I hear them telling the people what they want to hear so the people will vote them in as their representatives. When I listen to talk radio I hear the media making excuses to justify cover ups. I know I'm not the only one.

The founders of this country knew the meaning of revolution. They knew the meaning of resistance and resilience. The Declaration of Independence is one of the greatest Revolutionary Documents ever written. They were talking about what I'm expressing in this poem. They were tired, motivated, ready, and willing to risk their lives.

"Galvanized"

Galvanized!!!

Revolutionize!!!

Open Minds!!!

Open eyes!!!

Diversify

Rally the people

Give them something to believe in

Spark Though

Ignite change

Make a difference

Spread Love

Speak the Truth

Fight to be Free

Stand For Justice

Make the sacrifices others aren't willing to make

Don't be afraid of the odds

Don't be afraid to correct what's wrong

Don't be afraid of leadership

Don't be afraid to make a choice

Use your platform

Use your gifts

Why neglect your passion?

Why neglect your people?

Why neglect your purpose?

Why neglect yourself?

<u>Every Man</u>

Throughout my life my enemies made me better. They made me strengthen myself. Because of my enemies I have learned to endure, educate, and overcome.

Having things to go up against brings the best out of me. My biggest enemy is this life sentence, and it's been a battle for the last 13 years. Alhamdulilah (All praise due to Allah) hasn't gotten the best of me. Spiritually, mentallym and physically I've had the upper hand thus far. However, if I'm not careful things can change at any time.

In certain parts of my life I was my biggest enemy. Winning that battle took time. Honestly, I didn't begin to win that battle until I realized by being my own enemy I was contributing to my own demise.

My whole life I've been against the odds. I used to tell my homies "A man can't understand pressure if he can't stand under pressure. With this country being the way it is we live underpressure. We have to embrace it (see it for what it is) before we can defeat it.

"Every Man"

Every man needs a enemy

Every man needs a reason to struggle

Every man needs a reason to fight

Every man needs something to conquer

Every man needs challenges

Every man need something to stand For

Every man need something to Live For

Every man need something to die For

Our enemies make us better

Our struggle make us stronger

Our Fights make us tougher

We conquer to never be conquered

We defeat the Fear of every challenge we meet

We stand For our belief

We live For our purpose

We die For our cause

To a man survival isn't a choice

Failure isn't an option

Men respect courage

Cowards respect Fear

<u>Fight</u>

To fight is to put forth a determined effort. It is to take a stand, to take a knee, to take a seat, and to refuse to move. When you fight you let it be known you are not okay with what's going on. You're knowing your defiance, your boldness, and resistance. There comes a time in all our lives when fighting isn't optional and it's obligatory.

All fights are not bloody contests. Some of the most significant fights involve no blood shed. Those one the types of fights that everyone can participate in. The kind of fights that have an empowering impact on humanity. Some of the fights I'm talking about are fighting against ignorance, fighting against poverty, fighting against addiction. Fights that will truly make a difference in someone's life.

"Fight"

Fight!

Resist!

Take to the field

Why look the other way

you scared to die?

What you living For?

George died in pursuit

Malcom died at the podium

Che died on his feet

Huey died in the street

We still at war

You think we not?

Look around you

Look at the prisons

Listen to the politicians

Watch the news

Read the paper

It's blatant

Now....

Ask yourself

What can you do about it?

How can you help revolutionize and reform?

How can you help this world become a better place?

How can you make a change?

It's easy

By fighting for what you believe is right

By resisting the urge to do anything else

How Many

Every person has a breaking point. Some people can tolerate more than others. It's really about the person, what they've been through, and what they're doing. When I see what is going on around America it makes me want to be in the streets rallying the people. It makes me want to organize communities. It makes me want to revolutionize and reform.

Throughout my life it hasn't taken much for me to get involved. When I see people being wronged, oppressed, and taken advantage of it's hard for me to resist the urge to help them. People have told me I should mind my business or just focus on me. My question to them is: How many times do they have to see injustice before they're ready to do something about it?

What a lot of people say to themselves is they came into this world by themselves. Indeed, however, the moment we came into this world we were surrounded by people there to help us. It's only right we repay the favor.

"How Many"

How many people have to die before we stand up?
How many mother's have to cry before we're Fed up?
How many children have to ask why before we man up?

I hope it's not too many more

We all know the History of Blacks in America

Denigrated because our skin wasn't Fair enough

Humiliated when our women were taken advantage of

Manipulated because our minds were shackled up

Enough is enough

We were given Feet to stand For something

We were given hands to fight For something

We were given minds to believe in something

We were given hearts to Live For something

Too many times the oppressed become the oppressor

Doing to others what was done to them

Let's be better?

What makes one person better than another

has nothing to do with skin color

It's about how you Treat people

What you teach people and How you reach people

It's about how you see people and having compassion For each other

It's about you

<u>Do it</u>

We're in a position to do things our ancestors couldn't. When I say I'm not just speaking about "Black American" I'm speaking about all Americans. Platforms are universal so voices can be heard all over. Because of social media, what we do can be seen all over. Let's make the most of these resources to unite around common causes.

We all have something we can contribute to making a change. That is one of the things that makes America and the world at large so diverse. We can not be afraid of the critics. When you have the heart and capabilities to do something that will have an impact (on someone or everyone) do it. YOu never know how much of what you do can inspire someone else to do it too.

"Do It"

Do it For the ones that couldn't

Do it For the ones that suffered and cried tears

Do it For the ones that were raped and brutalized For years

Do it For the ones that hoped and For the ones that prayed

Do it For the ones that were to scared to run so they stayed

Do it For the Many

Do it For the Few

Do it For the ones that look like me and you

Do it to Re- Educate the ones that look like them

Do it For her

Do it For him

Do it For the Children

Do it For the Women

Do it For the Brother's and Sister's locked away in prison

(We Love Yall)

Do it For the ones without a voice

Do it For the one without a choice

Do it For the Jobless

Do it For the Homeless

Do it For your Family

Do it For Yourself

Do it

Do What?

Make a Change

The Leader

The key concept of leadership is influence. Being influential is a byproduct of having credibility. When you're a good example and a good representation people will listen to you. When you're known for getting good results and bringing life to your group people will follow you. That can be applied to anything.

The higher the stakes the more reliable the leader must be. The leader isn't the one who just stands out in front. Leadership is about action. If I'm leading you that means you're making the moves I make and you're taking the steps I take. Leadership should be earned. Be a leader by your actions not by your title.

Every position of leadership I've held came from my abilities to educate, organize, develop, inspire, and engage. I'm still learning a lot about being a leader. At times it's challenging, however, I can't turn away. Everything I've lived through has shown me this is my role among men.

"The Leader"

The leader is the Ideal

The Leader is the standard of excellence

The Leader embodies the principles, creed, and mentality of his cause

The Leader set the tone of conduct and characteristics

The Leader prescribes the optimum For Growth and Development

The Leader make the ultimate sacrifices

The Leader inspires Determination

What's a head without a body?

What's a body without a head?

The Leader is the Furthest away From collapsing

The Leader personify Discipline

He exercise his strengths

He never show his weakness

Therefore

His enemies never know his weakness

The Leader know the difference between patience and procrastination

The Leader empowers his soldiers

The Leader encourage his Troops

The Leader Motivate his Nation

The Leader is the Best example

The Leader never denies his responsibility

The Leader is the standard of excellence

The Leader is the Ideal

The Woman

The woman…

At her best

She's Elegant

She's Brilliant

She's Beautiful

She's a touch of God's grace

The tunnel of life

A timeless masterpiece

A priceless jewel

The Woman…

She deserves my Love

She deserves my Trust

She deserves my Respect

She deserves my Best

For her

Im Thankful

Her existence gives my life more meaning

She's delicate yet firm

Gentle yet strong

Severne yet sound

The Woman…

Throughout it all

She's resilient

She know what she want

She stand for what she believe

"For Majesty Pt.1"

Do your best

Make every minute count

Be your best

No one else can be the special girl you are

Listen and pay attention

The world is a classroom

You can learn something anywhere you go

Always Question what you don't understand

Don't be afraid to be different

Don't be afraid to be right when everyone else is wrong

The moon and the stars are so beautiful

because they shine in the Darkness

Be the one that makes things better

Don't Focus on the Problem

Focus on how to solve the problem

Majesty is Greatness

Majesty is Power

Majesty is Royalty

Majesty is You

For Majesty pt.2

To be special is to be unique

To be unique is to be one of a kind

To be one of a kind is to be Brilliant

To be brilliant is to shine bright like the sun

To shine bright like the sun is to be outstanding

To be outstanding is to be excellent

To be excellent is to be Great

All of this is you

You're special

You're unique

You're Brilliant

You're Outstanding

You're Excellent

You're Great

Never stop being you

Don't be afraid to be the leader

Don't be afraid to speak your mind

Trust yourself

Love yourself

Be sure of yourself

Take care of yourself

Set goals For yourself

Make Smart choices

Work hard

Be the Best you

"For B."

The bond we share is everlasting

In 9 months you built a temple of life we both cherish

My love For your significance Flow like the nile

You're the earth in my universe

The Mother of my child

I Honor you

I Respect you I Trust you For you

My appreciation re-define appreciation

Our energy can give power to the world

We bring light

You glow like the moon

I shine like the sun

Our connection resist suppression

We're together even we're apart

You're a queen in my kingdom

Without a doubt

If the price of love was Dealt

I'll die twice

Just to show you

Im thankful

"For someone special"

When I see you

I see hope

I see ambition

I see strength

I see undeniable beauty

I see potential

I see brilliance

I see someone that can make a difference

I see someone brave enough to stand up for what's right

I see someone bold enough to go against the odds

I see courage

I see confidence

I see class

I see sassiness

I see a light that can dazzle the darkness

Simply put

When I see you

I see what I like

I see a lot of purpose

I see a lot of good

I see alot of quality

Of Course my eyes could be deceiving me

But …

I don't think they are

Appreciation

(dedicated to someone special)

In this world

Appreciation is a token of Honor

It means your words have merit

It means your presence have value

It means your effort is noticeable

In many ways

Appreciation signifies your importance

It signifies esteem

Appreciation is earned it's not entitled

To be appreciated is to be held in high regard

Therefore

Appreciation should humble you

It should encourage you

It should empower you

Without doubt

A little help can make a big difference

From me to you

Continue to be you

Continue to care

Continue to be helpful

Continue to be special

Continue to let your light shine through what you do

And know

You are appreciated

"Life can change at anytime"

It has a beginning so it will end

Nevertheless

Love is everlasting

It's boundless

It's infinite

When it's real

It's unconditional

Some say Love is an emotion

I disagree

Emotions change

Love Don't

When you love you love Forever

If it's not Forever

It's wasn't Love in the beginning

After you go

Love keeps you alive

Love bring Joyous memories

When we Focus on Love

We gain From what we lose

Because we understand

Life can change at anytime

It has a beginning so it will end

Nevertheless

Love is everlasting

F.O.C.U.S

Fix: To Fix is to direct steadily, Establish, assign or adjust. In life whatever the mind is Fixed on it will achieve, manifest, build, or destroy. When we give our energy to something it transforms our energy into action. That action creates a response or reaction that will advance, retain or reverse us. In order to perform at your fullest potential you have to direct your-self properly through whatever it may be. Not fixing your attention on the matter at hand can cause detrimental effects, especially when it's a serious situation. The person that doesn't adjust their mind to see through all shades of darkness will always be blind to the facts.

Observe: Ignorance is the means of un-productive ends. The person that doesn't observe isn't aware; awareness is vital. Being watchful is beneficial in more than one way; You study, analyze, and listen by watching. The moment you fail to pay attention can be the moment you lose everything you have in front of you. The smallest detail can make the biggest difference.

Center: Everything in this universe came from a source and this source is the center of creation. When something is centered it's the core that keeps everything around it in harmony. We can apply this concept to ourselves to be more important to our environment. To be self- centered is to be concerned with only yourself. To center yourself is to place yourself in the core of every beneficial thing you have going on. The man who places himself in the middle of something to maintain order is not only courageous and selfless; he's also qualified to lead the people.

Utilize: The person who doesn't use the resources they have to better their life is just as useless as the resources. Having an advantage alone is not enough. You must know how to use the advantage to get the full benefit. In order to make something out of nothing you have to be able to force nothing to become something. Some of the most useful things we have are natural; they cost nothing but development. Yet, people often neglect their natural capabilities. TImes will get harder and circumstances will get worse if we don't utilize ourselves (and other resources) to make our lives better. Use what you have to get more of what you need to succeed; once you do succeed, teach others how to do it.

Stability: The ability to endure and remain in a constant state is a strength within itself. Distractions only become Distractions when we allow them too. Longevity is the goal; when something is firmly established it's established to withstand any and all forms of failure. A continuous reminder will assist you in remaining consistent due to the fact repetition is the Father of learning. In this world of cares what's not stabilized will be blown away when the wind of illusions cause a hell storm in the heart of man.

Printed in the United States
by Baker & Taylor Publisher Services